The Riverside Literature Series

STICKEEN

THE STORY OF A DOG

BY

JOHN MUIR

WITH INTRODUCTION AND NOTES BY
FRANCIS H. ALLEN

BOSTON NEW YORK CHICAGO
HOUGHTON MIFFLIN COMPANY
The Riverside Press Cambridge

The Riverside Press
CAMBRIDGE . MASSACHUSETTS
U . S . A

JOHN MUIR

John Muir was born April 21, 1838, at Dunbar, Scotland, about twenty-five miles from Edinburgh. He was the third child and the eldest son of Daniel and Anne (Gilrye) Muir. In his *Story of My Boyhood and Youth* he has given a vivid account of his childhood there on the shore of the North Sea, — of his schooling and the schoolboy fights which were so common as to seem almost a regular part of the curriculum, of rambles in the woods and along the shore, and deeds of daring known as "scootchers" in which the boys vied with one another in the most reckless performances.

John Muir was born with even more than the usual boy's love of wildness, and when, at the age of eleven, his father emigrated to America, he looked forward with eagerness to the new life in the American forests. It was in Wisconsin

John Muir

that Daniel Muir settled, in Marquette County, about a dozen miles north of Portage, the nearest town, and there he cleared the land for a farm, which became the family home for eight years, at the end of which time he moved four or five miles to the eastward and cleared another farm there. The boy delighted in the birds and other wild creatures of the woods and waters, but he had little time for roaming, for his father believed in hard work for himself and others, and, indeed, hard work was a necessity in subduing the wilderness. John was set at ploughing when he was only twelve years old, and for many years he did most of the ploughing required on the farm. He split rails for fences, too, like Abraham Lincoln, and came to be able to split a hundred oak rails in a day. By the time he was sixteen he led all the hired men on the farm in mowing and cradling.

John Muir

When he was about fifteen he began to feel a hunger for knowledge. He borrowed books of the neighbors and saved up and bought some for himself. He read till bedtime, which came all too soon after supper, and as much longer as he could. His father, who, though a kind-hearted man, was a strict disciplinarian and as an old-fashioned Calvinist believed that the only knowledge good for man was contained in the Bible, insisted on his going to bed with the rest of the family, but once unwarily added: "If you *will* read, get up in the morning and read. You may get up in the morning as early as you like." After that early rising was the order of the boy's day, much to the dismay of the father. In these early morning hours he worked on various ingenious machines of his own invention, — such as a wooden clock to tip one out of bed when the time for rising came, — and after he had accumulated a number of these, he followed the advice of a neighbor and took them to the State Fair at Madison, where they attracted much attention. He was then twenty-two years old. At Madison he received and accepted an offer of work in a machine-shop at Prairie du Chien, Wisconsin, but after a short time there he returned to Madison to work his way through the State University. This he accomplished by harvesting and teaching and in other ways.

He spent four years at the University, but did not take the regular course, specializing instead in chemistry, mathematics, physics, botany, and geology, with a little Latin and Greek, and when he left it, it was, as he expressed it, "only leaving one University for another, the Wisconsin University for the University of the Wilderness." He was, indeed,

John Muir

always learning, and only a few years before his death, in filling out a paper of biographical information, he described himself as a " student."

Students, like other people, must be fed and clothed, and John Muir's mechanical ingenuity was soon turned to account to earn him a living. From 1865 to 1867 he was employed in a woodworking factory at Trout's Mills, near Meaford, Ontario, on the shore of the Georgian Bay of Lake Huron, but all this while his heart was set on travel and natural science, and in 1866, in a letter to a botanist friend, he exclaimed, " How intensely I desire to be a Humboldt ! " The jog that started him on his career came in March, 1867, in the form of a serious accident to one of his eyes from an implement in his own hand. This forced him to stop work for a time. During his convalescence he went to Indianapolis,

John Muir

where he had lived for a year or so after leaving college, and thence he started out in June on a botanizing trip to Illinois and Wisconsin. He returned to Indianapolis in August, but early in September began a long walking trip, which took him through Indiana, Kentucky, Tennessee, Georgia, and Florida. In Florida he was seized with a severe attack of malarial fever, and while recovering, he visited Cuba, where he spent four weeks in January and February, 1868. Still desiring to be a Humboldt, he had planned an exploration of the upper waters of the Amazon, but his weakened condition forbade, and he took the less hazardous trip from Cuba to California, crossing the Isthmus by rail and taking ship to San Francisco, where he arrived in April. Thence he proceeded on foot to the Yosemite, there to find his life work and the home of his spirit, though it was not till the fol-

John Muir

lowing year that he took up his residence there.

To form any conception of what the Yosemite Valley and the high Sierra above it meant to John Muir, the reader must go to his books. No geologist and botanist who is not also a poet, no poet who is not also a naturalist, can appreciate it fully. Here at Yosemite Muir spent five whole years and five more summers. At first he earned his living superintending a flock of sheep, then he built a sawmill and worked it, sawing fallen trees only, for he loved the forest too dearly to dismember it. But his wants were few. On a little bread and a little tea he would make long foot journeys alone over the Sierra, sometimes for weeks at a time without returning to his base. He slept out without a tent where night found him, and it is related that once, overtaken by a sudden snowstorm, he made a bed in a drift and lived there for three days like a bear in his den, with only a few crackers, some cheese, and, by luck, a bit of bacon for sustenance.

At first he devoted himself chiefly to botany, but the great problem of the geological formation of the valley forced itself upon his attention and soon became his principal study. On one glorious day, when he found a living glacier among the surrounding mountains, he realized that the problem was solved. It was some time before he succeeded in convincing the professional geologists that Yosemite had been formed by glacial action, but the day came when they all admitted it. Agassiz, famous for his work in proving the existence of the vast continental glaciers, said, "No man living understands glacial action in the formation of scenery as that young Muir in California."

Many well-known men, philosophers

John Muir

and scientists and poets, visited John Muir at Yosemite. Agassiz, to Muir's disappointment, was unable to go there when he visited California. Emerson came, and the two men delighted in each other's company, though it was a source of lasting regret to Muir that Emerson's companions would not allow the philosopher, who was then old and in delicate health, to sleep in the forest.

From 1876 to 1878 Muir was a member of an exploring party on the geodetic survey of the Great Basin, and in 1879 he made the first of his trips to Alaska, the one in which he discovered the huge glacier which is now known by his name. It was on his second visit to Alaska, in the following year, that the incident occurred which is related in his story of *Stickeen*. He visited the glaciers of Alaska again in 1890, and in 1899 he was a member of the Harriman

John Muir

Expedition, which explored the coast of Alaska, the Aleutian Islands, and Behring Sea. Mr. John Burroughs and other noted men were also of the Harriman expedition, which was financed and conducted by Mr. E. H. Harriman, the "railroad king." Meanwhile, in 1881, John Muir had accompanied in the capacity of botanist the Corwin expedition through Behring Sea and the Arctic Ocean in search of the lost Arctic explorer De Long and his ship the Jeannette. In 1880 he had married Louise, the daughter of Dr. John Strentzel, of California, and the ranch at Martinez, California, which she inherited, was his home for many years before his death.

John Muir made occasional trips to the Eastern States, and in 1893 he went to Europe, visiting his birthplace in Scotland and traveling through the Alps and Norway. In 1897 he was a member

John Muir

of the United States Forest Commission.
He went round the world in 1903–04,
traveling in Russia, Siberia, Manchuria,
India, Australia, and New Zealand, and
he visited South America in 1911 and
South Africa in 1911–12. These ex-
tensive travels were chiefly for the study
of the trees of these countries. When
he was not traveling, Mr. Muir devoted
himself during these later years to the
management of his fruit ranch at Martinez and to writing. His first book,
The Mountains of California, was published in 1894, and this was followed by
Our National Parks in 1901, *Stickeen*
in 1909, *My First Summer in the Sierra*
in 1911, *The Yosemite* in 1912, and
The Story of My Boyhood and Youth in
1913. A posthumous volume, *Travels in
Alaska*, was published in 1915. He was
active till within a short time of his death,
and among the last of his activities was

John Muir

the losing fight he conducted against the alienation of the Hetch-Hetchy Valley from the Yosemite National Park. The loss of this battle and the delivery of that beautiful valley to form a part of San Francisco's water-system was a great blow to him, physically as well as in spirit. He caught a severe cold while away from home, and was taken to Los Angeles, where his malady developed into pneumonia, from which he died, December 24, 1914.

John Muir will always rank as one of the greatest of American writers on nature. He has been called the Thoreau of the West, and he has been likened to John Burroughs, but he was neither a Thoreau nor a Burroughs. He was very different from either of those two men, a sincere and whole-souled love of nature being about all he had in common with

John Muir

them. In Muir this love of nature took the form of a high and reverent enthusiasm. His father was a religious enthusiast of the old Scotch Presbyterian type. It was a stern and rather gloomy enthusiasm for the most part with him, though a wonderful aurora awoke him to exclamations on the glory of God. The son had all the enthusiasm, and more, with none of the gloom of the traditional Scottish theology. He was intensely religious, but his view of life was broadened by his scientific education and interests, and his temperament was buoyant.

This enthusiasm of John Muir's as he writes of the mountains and forests and glaciers which he loves is catching and is an important element in the charm of his books. It is not all, however. There is sincerity besides, and keenness of perception, an eye for color and form, an ear for the elemental sounds of nature, a faculty for description. He was not an easy writer, we are told. He labored over his literary work, revising and polishing till it suited him, but the reader does not suspect this, for his sentences seem always to flow as freely as the streams run down his mountain valleys.

Delightful as he was, and is, as a writer, Mr. Muir was, if anything, still more delightful in conversation. He had the simplicity which belongs to men who have lived much alone out of doors, and his enthusiastic habit of mind carried him along in a stream of talk which his hearers were generally only too glad to allow to become a monologue. He could entertain a roomful of strangers with accounts of his mountaineering adventures with perfect simplicity and with no more self-consciousness than one would feel in a private conversation with a friend or two by one's own fireside. In more in-

John Muir

timate relations he was a "born tease,"
and he delighted to take his friends
"down a peg" when he thought it ad-
visable, all with the greatest good humor.
In his *Story of My Boyhood and Youth*
he tells how, at the age of two and a half,
he once bit his tongue severely, and
when, in his sleep, he had swallowed the
wad of medicated cotton the doctor had
pushed into his mouth, he imagined he
had swallowed the tongue too. After-
wards, when his sisters thought he was
talking too much, they would remind
him of the incident and express regret
that he had not swallowed at least half
of that long tongue of his when he was
little.. Few, however, who were privi-
leged to hear his conversation after he
had grown up would have echoed that
sentiment, though it cannot be denied
that his tongue was always a long one,
and sharp too at times.

John Muir

John Muir was early interested in birds and birds' nests, as, indeed, the other little Scotch boys were, and when he first found himself birds'-nesting in the woods of Wisconsin, he was " utterly happy." He never lost this interest, and one of his best essays — one of the most delightful bird-sketches in all literature — is his chapter on the water-ousel, or dipper, in *The Mountains of California*. He made no deliberate study of birds, however, and, as Theodore Roosevelt has said, he paid little attention to them unless some unusual trait or habit attracted his notice. When President Roosevelt visited him at Yosemite and remarked on the thrushes which were singing all about them at the time, he found to his surprise that Muir had not even heard them and did not know to what species they belonged.

John Muir loved and respected all wild life. He bore no grudge even against

John Muir

venomous reptiles, and when he found a rattlesnake in his path, he walked round it and left it undisturbed in the enjoyment of its existence. In his view all the animals led happy lives. When he saw the great whales ploughing the Pacific, he thought of the joy they must feel as each beat of their mighty hearts sent the warm blood coursing through their bodies by the barrelful. With his feeling of comradeship with animals of all kinds he had no desire to take life. He was never a hunter nor a fisherman, and flesh-eating was distasteful to him. His books are full of the beauty and joy that he found in nature.

To communicate to his readers so much of the beauty and joy of life in the woods and on the mountains would have been service enough to his fellow men, but this was by no means all of John Muir's service to his country and the

John Muir

world. His discoveries in glacial geology were important contributions to science, and his successful work in the conservation of forests and scenery should make his name glorious among all Americans who love their country. It was he who saved the Big Trees of the General Grant National Park, and it was largely his work that the Yosemite National Park was established in 1890. He was one of the founders in 1892 of the Sierra Club, a potent influence in conservation, and was its president as long as he lived. He was also at the time of his death president of the Society for the Preservation of National Parks and vice-president of the California Associated Societies for the Conservation of Wild Life.

John Muir's love of wildness — and no man ever loved wild nature better — was no selfish passion. He hated the trivialities that many tourists take with them into the wilderness, but his written and spoken words were a constant invitation to all thoughtful persons to come into the mountains and see — come and see!

Stickeen is one of the best dog stories ever written. It is not merely a story of adventure with a dog for hero. (Indeed, in a strict sense, the little dog is no great hero after all.) But it opens a window into the heart and soul of a dog, so that we can see how much like a man he is in some respects and can sympathize with him. It is a great thing, sympathy. Without it we cannot understand our fellow creatures, human or animal, and the more we have of understanding and sympathy, the richer are our lives. With sympathy and understanding we are never alone and lonely in this world so long as other living creatures are about

John Muir

us. If you feel inclined to think that any
dog you know — or any person — is
cold and heartless, or tiresome and un-
interesting, remember Stickeen.

TO MY DOG BLANCO

BY J. G. HOLLAND

My dear dumb friend, low lying there,
   A willing vassal at my feet;
Glad partner of my home and fare,
   My shadow in the street;

I look into your great brown eyes,
   Where love and loyal homage shine,
And wonder where the difference lies
   Between your soul and mine!

. . . . . .

I scan the whole broad earth around
   For that one heart which, leal and true,
Bears friendship without end or bound,
   And find the prize in you.

. . . . . .

Ah, Blanco! did I worship God
   As truly as you worship me,
Or follow where my Master trod
   With your humility:

Did I sit fondly at His feet
 As you, dear Blanco, sit at mine,
And watch Him with a love as sweet,
 My life would grow divine!

STICKEEN

STICKEEN

IN the summer of 1880 I set out from Fort Wrangel in a canoe to continue the exploration of the icy region of southeastern Alaska, begun in the fall of 1879. After the necessary provisions, blankets, etc., had been collected and stowed away, and my Indian crew were in their places ready to start, while a crowd of their relatives and friends on the wharf were bidding them good-by and good-luck, my companion, the Rev. S. H. Young, for whom we were waiting, at last came aboard, followed by a little black dog, that immediately made himself at home by curling up in a hollow among the baggage. I like dogs, but this one seemed so small and worthless that I objected to his going, and asked the missionary why he was taking him.

"Such a little helpless creature will only be in the way," I said; "you had better pass him up to the Indian boys on the wharf, to be taken home to play with the children. This trip is not likely to be good for toy-dogs. The poor silly thing will be in rain and snow for weeks or months, and will require care like a baby."

But his master assured me that he would be no trouble at all; that he

[4]

Stickeen

was a perfect wonder of a dog, could endure cold and hunger like a bear, swim like a seal, and was wondrous wise and cunning, etc., making out a list of virtues to show he might be the most interesting member of the party.

Nobody could hope to unravel the lines of his ancestry. In all the wonderfully mixed and varied dog-tribe I never saw any creature very much like him, though in some of his sly, soft, gliding motions and gestures he brought the fox to mind. He was short-legged and bunchy-bodied, and his hair, though smooth, was long and silky and slightly waved, so that when the wind was at his back it ruffled, making him look shaggy. At first sight his only noticeable feature was his fine tail, which was about as airy and shady as a squirrel's, and was carried curling forward almost to his nose. On closer inspection you might notice his thin sensitive ears, and sharp eyes with cunning tan-spots above them. Mr. Young told me that when the little fellow was a pup about the size of a woodrat he was presented to his wife by an Irish prospector at Sitka, and that on his arrival at Fort Wrangel he was adopted with enthusiasm by the Stickeen Indians as a sort of new good-luck totem, was named "Stickeen" for the tribe, and became a universal favorite; petted, protected, and admired wherever he went, and regarded as a mysterious fountain of wisdom.

On our trip he soon proved himself a queer character — odd, concealed, independent, keeping invincibly quiet, and doing many little puzzling things that piqued my curiosity. As we sailed week after week through the long intricate channels and inlets among the innumerable islands and mountains of the coast, he spent most of the dull days in sluggish ease, motionless, and apparently as unobserving as if in deep sleep. But I discovered that somehow he always knew what was going on. When the Indians were about to shoot at ducks or seals, or when anything along the shore was exciting our attention, he would rest his chin on the edge of the canoe and calmly look out like a dreamy-eyed tourist. And when he heard us talking about making a landing, he immediately roused himself to see what sort of a place we were coming to, and made ready to jump overboard and swim ashore as soon as the canoe neared the beach. Then, with a vigorous shake to get rid of the brine in his hair, he ran into the woods to hunt small game. But though always the first out of the canoe, he was always the last to get into it. When we were ready to start he could never be found, and refused to come to our call. We soon found out, however, that though we could not see him at such times, he saw us, and from the cover of the briers and huckleberry bushes in the fringe of the woods was watching the canoe with wary eye. For as soon as we were fairly off he came trotting down the beach, plunged into the surf, and swam after us, knowing well that we would cease rowing and take him in. When the contrary little vagabond came alongside, he was lifted by the neck, held at arm's length a moment to drip, and dropped aboard. We tried to cure him of this trick by compelling him to swim a long way, as if we had a mind to abandon him; but this did no good: the longer the swim the better he seemed to like it.

Though capable of great idleness, he never failed to be ready for all sorts of adventures and excursions. One pitch‑dark rainy night we landed about ten o'clock at the mouth of a salmon stream when the water was phosphorescent. The salmon were running, and the myriad fins of the onrushing multitude were churning all the stream into a silvery glow, wonderfully beautiful and impressive in the ebon darkness. To get a good

view of the show I set out with one of
the Indians and sailed up through the
midst of it to the foot of a rapid about
half a mile from camp, where the swift
current dashing over rocks made the
luminous glow most glorious. Hap-
pening to look back down the stream,
while the Indian was catching a few
of the struggling fish, I saw a long
spreading fan of light like the tail of
a comet, which we thought must be
made by some big strange animal that
was pursuing us. On it came with its
magnificent train, until we imagined
we could see the monster's head and
eyes; but it was only Stickeen, who,
finding I had left the camp, came

swimming after me to see what was up.

When we camped early, the best hunter of the crew usually went to the woods for a deer, and Stickeen was sure to be at his heels, provided I had not gone out. For, strange to say, though I never carried a gun, he always followed me, forsaking the hunter and even his master to share my wanderings. The days that were too stormy for sailing I spent in the woods, or on the adjacent mountains, wherever my studies called me; and Stickeen always insisted on going with me, however wild the weather, gliding like a fox through dripping huckleberry bushes and thorny tangles of panax and rubus, scarce stirring their rain-laden leaves; wading and wallowing through snow, swimming icy streams, skipping over logs and rocks and the crevasses of glaciers with the patience and endurance of a determined mountaineer, never tiring or getting discouraged. Once he followed me over a glacier the surface of which was so crusty and rough that it cut his feet until every step was marked with blood; but he trotted on with Indian fortitude until I noticed his red track, and, taking pity on him, made him a set of moccasins out of a handkerchief. However great his troubles he never asked help or made any complaint, as if, like a philosopher, he had learned that without hard work and suffering there could be no pleasure worth having.

Yet none of us was able to make out what Stickeen was really good for. He seemed to meet danger and hardships without anything like reason, insisted on having his own way, never obeyed an order, and the hunter could never set him on anything, or make him fetch the birds he shot. His equanimity was so steady it seemed due to want of feeling; ordinary storms were pleasures to him, and as for mere rain, he flourished in it like a vegetable.

Stickeen

No matter what advances you might make, scarce a glance or a tail-wag would you get for your pains. But though he was apparently as cold as a glacier and about as impervious to fun, I tried hard to make his acquaintance, guessing there must be something worth while hidden beneath so much courage, endurance, and love of wild-weathery adventure. No superannuated mastiff or bulldog grown old in office surpassed this fluffy midget in stoic dignity. He sometimes reminded me of a small, squat, unshakable desert cactus. For he never displayed a single trace of the merry, tricksy, elfish fun of the terriers and collies that we

all know, nor of their touching affec-
tion and devotion. Like children, most
small dogs beg to be loved and al-
lowed to love; but Stickeen seemed a
very Diogenes, asking only to be let
alone: a true child of the wilderness,
holding the even tenor of his hidden
life with the silence and serenity of
nature. His strength of character lay
in his eyes. They looked as old as the
hills, and as young, and as wild. I
never tired of looking into them : it
was like looking into a landscape;
but they were small and rather deep-
set, and had no explaining lines
around them to give out particulars. I
was accustomed to look into the faces

of plants and animals, and I watched the little sphinx more and more keenly as an interesting study. But there is no estimating the wit and wisdom concealed and latent in our lower fellow mortals until made manifest by profound experiences; for it is through suffering that dogs as well as saints are developed and made perfect.

After exploring the Sumdum and Tahkoo fiords and their glaciers, we sailed through Stephen's Passage into Lynn Canal and thence through Icy Strait into Cross Sound, searching for unexplored inlets leading toward the great fountain ice-fields of the Fairweather Range. Here, while the tide was in our favor, we were accompanied by a fleet of icebergs drifting out to the ocean from Glacier Bay. Slowly we paddled around Vancouver's Point, Wimbledon, our frail canoe tossed like a feather on the massive heaving swells coming in past Cape Spenser. For miles the sound is bounded by precipitous mural cliffs, which, lashed with wave-spray and their heads hidden in clouds, looked terribly threatening and stern. Had our canoe been crushed or upset we could have made no landing here, for the cliffs, as high as those of Yosemite, sink sheer into deep water. Eagerly we scanned the wall on the north side for the first sign of an opening fiord or harbor, all of us anxious except Stickeen, who dozed in peace or gazed dreamily at the tremendous precipices when he heard us talking about them. At length we made the joyful discovery of the mouth of the inlet now called "Taylor Bay," and about five o'clock reached the head of it and encamped in a spruce grove near the front of a large glacier.

While camp was being made, Joe the hunter climbed the mountain wall on the east side of the fiord in pursuit of wild goats, while Mr. Young and I went to the glacier. We found that it is separated from the waters of the inlet by a tide-washed moraine, and extends, an abrupt barrier, all the way across from wall to wall of the inlet, a distance of about three miles. But our most interesting discovery was that it had recently advanced, though again slightly receding. A portion of the terminal moraine had been plowed up and shoved forward, uprooting and overwhelming the woods on the east side. Many of the trees were down and buried, or nearly so, others were leaning away from the ice-cliffs, ready to fall, and some stood erect, with the bottom of the ice plow still beneath their roots and its lofty crystal spires towering high above their tops. The spectacle presented by these century-old trees standing close beside a spiry wall of ice, with their branches almost touching it, was most novel and striking. And when I climbed around the front, and a little way up the west side of the glacier, I found that it had swelled and increased in height and width in accordance with its advance, and carried away the outer ranks of trees on its bank.

On our way back to camp after these first observations I planned a far-and-wide excursion for the morrow. I awoke early, called not only by the glacier, which had been on my mind all night, but by a grand flood-

storm. The wind was blowing a gale
from the north and the rain was flying with the clouds in a wide passionate horizontal flood, as if it were all
passing over the country instead of
falling on it. The main perennial
streams were booming high above
their banks, and hundreds of new
ones, roaring like the sea, almost cov-
ered the lofty gray walls of the inlet
with white cascades and falls. I had
intended making a cup of coffee and
getting something like a breakfast
before starting, but when I heard the
storm and looked out I made haste to
join it; for many of Nature's finest
lessons are to be found in her storms,

and if careful to keep in right relations with them, we may go safely
abroad with them, rejoicing in the
grandeur and beauty of their works
and ways, and chanting with the old
Norsemen, "The blast of the tem-
pest aids our oars, the hurricane is
our servant and drives us whither we
wish to go." So, omitting breakfast,
I put a piece of bread in my pocket
and hurried away.

Mr. Young and the Indians were
asleep, and so, I hoped, was Stickeen;
but I had not gone a dozen rods before
he left his bed in the tent and came
boring through the blast after me.
That a man should welcome storms

for their exhilarating music and motion, and go forth to see God making landscapes, is reasonable enough ; but what fascination could there be in such tremendous weather for a dog? Surely nothing akin to human enthusiasm for scenery or geology. Anyhow, on he came, breakfastless, through the choking blast. I stopped and did my best to turn him back. "Now don't," I said, shouting to make myself heard in the storm, "now don't, Stickeen. What has got into your queer noddle now? You must be daft. This wild day has nothing for you. There is no game abroad, nothing but weather. Go back to camp and keep

warm, get a good breakfast with your
master, and be sensible for once. I
can't carry you all day or feed you,
and this storm will kill you."

But Nature, it seems, was at the
bottom of the affair, and she gains her
ends with dogs as well as with men,
making us do as she likes, shoving
and pulling us along her ways, however rough, all but killing us at times
in getting her lessons driven hard
home. After I had stopped again and
again, shouting good warning advice,
I saw that he was not to be shaken
off; as well might the earth try to
shake off the moon. I had once led his
master into trouble, when he fell on

one of the topmost jags of a mountain
and dislocated his arm; now the turn
of his humble companion was coming. The pitiful little wanderer just
stood there in the wind, drenched and
blinking, saying doggedly, "Where
thou goest I will go." So at last I told
him to come on if he must, and gave
him a piece of the bread I had in my
pocket; then we struggled on together, and thus began the most
memorable of all my wild days.

The level flood, driving hard in our
faces, thrashed and washed us wildly
until we got into the shelter of a
grove on the east side of the glacier
near the front, where we stopped

awhile for breath and to listen and look out. The exploration of the glacier was my main object, but the wind was too high to allow excursions over its open surface, where one might be dangerously shoved while balancing for a jump on the brink of a crevasse. In the mean time the storm was a fine study. Here the end of the glacier, descending an abrupt swell of resisting rock about five hundred feet high, leans forward and falls in ice cascades. And as the storm came down the glacier from the north, Stickeen and I were beneath the main current of the blast, while favorably located to see and hear it. What a psalm the storm

was singing, and how fresh the smell
of the washed earth and leaves, and
how sweet the still small voices of
the storm! Detached wafts and swirls
were coming through the woods, with
music from the leaves and branches
and furrowed boles, and even from
the splintered rocks and ice-crags
overhead, many of the tones soft and
low and flute-like, as if each leaf and
tree, crag and spire were a tuned reed.
A broad torrent, draining the side of
the glacier, now swollen by scores
of new streams from the mountains,
was rolling boulders along its rocky
channel, with thudding, bumping,
muffled sounds, rushing towards the

bay with tremendous energy, as if in haste to get out of the mountains; the waters above and beneath calling to each other, and all to the ocean, their home.

Looking southward from our shelter, we had this great torrent and the forested mountain wall above it on our left, the spiry ice-crags on our right, and smooth gray gloom ahead. I tried to draw the marvelous scene in my note-book, but the rain blurred the page in spite of all my pains to shelter it, and the sketch was almost worthless. When the wind began to abate, I traced the east side of the glacier. All the trees standing on the edge of the woods were barked and bruised, showing high-ice mark in a very telling way, while tens of thousands of those that had stood for centuries on the bank of the glacier farther out lay crushed and being crushed. In many places I could see down fifty feet or so beneath the margin of the glacier-mill, where trunks from one to two feet in diameter were being ground to pulp against outstanding rock-ribs and bosses of the bank.

About three miles above the front of the glacier I climbed to the surface of it by means of axe-steps made easy for Stickeen. As far as the eye could reach, the level, or nearly level, gla-

cier stretched away indefinitely beneath the gray sky, a seemingly
boundless pr a e of ice. The rain con-
tinued, and grew colder, which I did
not mind, but a dim snowy look in
the drooping clouds made me hesitate
about venturing far from land. No
trace of the west shore was visible,
and in case the clouds should settle
and give snow, or the wind again become violent, I feared getting caught
in a tangle of crevasses. Snow-crys-
tals, the flowers of the mountain
clouds, are frail, beautiful things, but
terrible when flying on storm-winds
in darkening, benumbing swarms or
when welded together into glaciers

full of deadly crevasses. Watching the weather, I sauntered about on the crystal sea. For a mile or two out I found the ice remarkably safe. The marginal crevasses were mostly narrow, while the few wider ones were easily avoided by passing around them, and the clouds began to open here and there.

Thus encouraged, I at last pushed out for the other side; for Nature can make us do anything she likes. At first we made rapid progress, and the sky was not very threatening, while I took bearings occasionally with a pocket compass to enable me to find my way back more surely in case the storm should become blinding; but the structure lines of the glacier were my main guide. Toward the west side we came to a closely crevassed section in which we had to make long, narrow tacks and doublings, tracing the edges of tremendous transverse and longitudinal crevasses, many of which were from twenty to thirty feet wide, and perhaps a thousand feet deep — beautiful and awful. In working a way through them I was severely cautious, but Stickeen came on as unhesitating as the flying clouds. The widest crevasse that I could jump he would leap without so much as halting to take a look at it. The weather was now making quick changes, scattering bits of dazzling brightness through the wintry gloom; at rare intervals, when the sun broke forth wholly free, the glacier was seen from shore to shore with a bright array of encompassing mountains partly revealed, wearing the clouds as garments, while the prairie bloomed and sparkled with irised light from myriads of washed crystals. Then suddenly all the glorious show would be darkened and blotted out.

Stickeen seemed to care for none of these things, bright or dark, nor for the crevasses, wells, moulins, or swift flashing streams into which he

might fall. The little adventurer was
only about two years old, yet nothing seemed novel to him, nothing
daunted him. He showed neither cau-
tion nor curiosity, wonder nor fear,
but bravely trotted on as if glaciers
were playgrounds. His stout, muffled body seemed all one skipping
muscle, and it was truly wonderful to
see how swiftly and to all appearance
heedlessly he flashed across nerve-
trying chasms six or eight feet wide.
His courage was so unwavering that
it seemed to be due to dullness of
perception, as if he were only blindly
bold; and I kept warning him to be
careful. For we had been close com-

panions on so many wilderness trips that I had formed the habit of talking to him as if he were a boy and understood every word.

We gained the west shore in about three hours; the width of the glacier here being about seven miles. Then I pushed northward in order to see as far back as possible into the fountains of the Fairweather Mountains, in case the clouds should rise. The walking was easy along the margin of the forest, which, of course, like that on the other side, had been invaded and crushed by the swollen, overflowing glacier. In an hour or so, after passing a massive headland, we came suddenly on a branch of the glacier, which, in the form of a magnificent ice-cascade two miles wide, was pouring over the rim of the main basin in a westerly direction, its surface broken into wave-shaped blades and shattered blocks, suggesting the wildest updashing, heaving, plunging motion of a great river cataract. Tracing it down three or four miles, I found that it discharged into a lake, filling it with icebergs.

I would gladly have followed the lake outlet to tide-water, but the day was already far spent, and the threatening sky called for haste on the return trip to get off the ice before dark.

Stickeen

I decided therefore to go no farther, and, after taking a general view of the wonderful region, turned back, hoping to see it again under more favorable auspices. We made good speed up the cañon of the great ice-torrent, and out on the main glacier until we had left the west shore about two miles behind us. Here we got into a difficult network of crevasses, the gathering clouds began to drop misty fringes, and soon the dreaded snow came flying thick and fast. I now began to feel anxious about finding a way in the blurring storm. Stickeen showed no trace of fear. He was still the same silent, able little hero. I noticed, however, that after the storm-darkness came on he kept close up behind me. The snow urged us to make still greater haste, but at the same time hid our way. I pushed on as best I could, jumping innumerable crevasses, and for every hundred rods or so of direct advance traveling a mile in doubling up and down in the turmoil of chasms and dislocated ice-blocks. After an hour or two of this work we came to a series of longitudinal crevasses of appalling width, and almost straight and regular in trend, like immense furrows. These I traced with firm nerve, excited and strengthened by the danger, making wide jumps, poising cautiously on their dizzy edges after cutting hollows for my feet before making the spring, to avoid possible slipping or any uncertainty on the farther sides, where only one trial is granted —exercise at once frightful and inspiring. Stickeen followed seemingly without effort.

Many a mile we thus traveled, mostly up and down, making but little real headway in crossing, running instead of walking most of the time as the danger of being compelled to spend the night on the glacier became threatening. Stickeen seemed able for anything. Doubtless we could have weathered the storm for one night, dancing on a flat spot to keep from freezing, and I faced the threat without feeling anything like despair; but we were hungry and wet, and the wind from the mountains was still thick with snow and bitterly cold, so of course that night would have seemed a very long one. I could not see far enough through the blurring snow to judge in which general direction the least dangerous route lay, while the few dim, momentary glimpses I caught of mountains through rifts in the flying clouds were far from encouraging either as weather signs or as guides. I had simply to grope my way from crevasse to crevasse, holding a general direction by the ice-structure, which was not to be seen everywhere, and partly by the wind. Again and again I was put to my mettle, but Stickeen followed easily, his nerve apparently growing more unflinching as the danger increased. So it always is with mountaineers when hard beset. Running hard and jumping, holding every minute of the remaining daylight, poor as it was, precious, we doggedly persevered and tried to hope that every difficult crevasse we overcame would prove to be the last of its kind. But on the contrary, as we

advanced they became more deadly
trying.

At length our way was barred by
a very wide and straight crevasse,
which I traced rapidly northward a
mile or so without finding a crossing
or hope of one; then down the glacier about as far, to where it united
with another uncrossable crevasse.
In all this distance of perhaps two
miles there was only one place where
I could possibly jump it, but the width
of this jump was the utmost I dared
attempt, while the danger of slipping
on the farther side was so great that I
was loath to try it. Furthermore, the
side I was on was about a foot higher

than the other, and even with this advantage the crevasse seemed dangerously wide. One is liable to underes-
timate the width of crevasses where
the magnitudes in general are great.
I therefore stared at this one mighty
keenly, estimating its width and the
shape of the edge on the farther side,
until I thought that I could jump it if
necessary, but that in case I should be
compelled to jump back from the
lower side I might fail. Now, a cautious mountaineer seldom takes a step
on unknown ground which seems at
all dangerous that he cannot retrace
in case he should be stopped by un-
seen obstacles ahead. This is the rule

of mountaineers who live long, and, though in haste, I compelled myself to sit down and calmly deliberate before I broke it.

Retracing my devious path in imagination as if it were drawn on a chart, I saw that I was recrossing the glacier a mile or two farther up stream than the course pursued in the morning, and that I was now entangled in a section I had not before seen. Should I risk this dangerous jump, or try to regain the woods on the west shore, make a fire, and have only hunger to endure while waiting for a new day? I had already crossed so broad a stretch of dangerous ice that

I saw it would be difficult to get back
to the woods through the storm, before dark, and the attempt would
most likely result in a dismal night-
dance on the glacier; while just beyond the present barrier the surface
seemed more promising, and the east
shore was now perhaps about as near
as the west. I was therefore eager to
go on. But this wide jump was a
dreadful obstacle.

At length, because of the dangers
already behind me, I determined to
venture against those that might be
ahead, jumped and landed well, but
with so little to spare that I more than
ever dreaded being compelled to take

that jump back from the lower side. Stickeen followed, making nothing of it, and we ran eagerly forward, hoping we were leaving all our troubles behind. But within the distance of a few hundred yards we were stopped by the widest crevasse yet encountered. Of course I made haste to explore it, hoping all might yet be remedied by finding a bridge or a way around either end. About three-fourths of a mile upstream I found that it united with the one we had just crossed, as I feared it would. Then, tracing it down, I found it joined the same crevasse at the lower end also, maintaining throughout its whole course a width of forty to fifty feet. Thus to my dismay I discovered that we were on a narrow island about two miles long, with two barely possible ways of escape: one back by the way we came, the other ahead by an almost inaccessible sliver-bridge that crossed the great crevasse from near the middle of it!

After this nerve-trying discovery I ran back to the sliver-bridge and cautiously examined it. Crevasses, caused by strains from variations in the rate of motion of different parts of the glacier and convexities in the channel, are mere cracks when they first open, so narrow as hardly to admit the blade of a pocket-knife, and gradually widen according to the extent of the strain and the depth of the glacier. Now some of these cracks are interrupted, like the cracks in wood, and in opening, the strip of ice between overlapping ends is dragged out, and may maintain a continuous connection between the sides, just as the two sides of a slivered crack in wood that is being split are connected. Some crevasses remain open for months or even years, and by the melting of their sides continue to increase in width long after the opening strain has ceased; while the sliver-bridges, level on top at first and perfectly safe, are at length melted to thin, vertical, knife-edged blades, the upper portion being most exposed to the weather; and since the exposure is greatest in the middle, they at length curve downward like the cables of suspension bridges. This one was evidently very old, for it had been weathered and wasted until it was the most dangerous and inaccessible that ever lay in my way. The width of the crevasse was here about fifty feet, and the sliver crossing diagonally was about seventy feet long; its thin knife-edge near the middle was depressed twenty-five or thirty feet below the level of the glacier, and the upcurving

ends were attached to the sides eight
or ten feet below the brink. Getting
down the nearly vertical wall to the
end of the sliver and up the other side
were the main difficulties, and they
seemed all but insurmountable. Of the
many perils encountered in my years
of wandering on mountains and glaciers none seemed so plain and stern
and merciless as this. And it was presented when we were wet to the skin
and hungry, the sky dark with quick
driving snow, and the night near.
But we were forced to face it. It was
a tremendous necessity.

Beginning, not immediately above
the sunken end of the bridge, but a

little to one side, I cut a deep hollow on the brink for my knees to rest in. Then, leaning over, with my short-handled axe I cut a step sixteen or eighteen inches below, which on account of the sheerness of the wall was necessarily shallow. That step, however, was well made; its floor sloped slightly inward and formed a good hold for my heels. Then, slipping cautiously upon it, and crouching as low as possible, with my left side toward the wall, I steadied myself against the wind with my left hand in a slight notch, while with the right I cut other similar steps and notches in succession, guarding against losing balance by glinting of the axe, or by wind-gusts, for life and death were in every stroke and in the niceness of finish of every foothold.

After the end of the bridge was reached I chipped it down until I had made a level platform six or eight inches wide, and it was a trying thing to poise on this little slippery platform while bending over to get safely astride of the sliver. Crossing was then comparatively easy by chipping off the sharp edge with short, careful strokes, and hitching forward an inch or two at a time, keeping my balance with my knees pressed against the sides. The tremendous abyss on either hand I studiously ignored. To me the edge of that blue sliver was then all the world. But the most trying part of the adventure, after working my way across inch by inch and chipping another small platform, was to rise from the safe position astride and to cut a step-ladder in the nearly vertical face of the wall, — chipping, climbing, holding on with feet and fingers in mere notches. At such times one's whole body is eye, and common skill and fortitude are replaced by power beyond our call or knowledge. Never before had I been so long under deadly strain. How I got up that cliff I never could tell. The thing seemed to have been done by somebody else. I never have held death in contempt, though in the course of my explorations I have oftentimes felt that to meet one's fate on a noble mountain, or in the heart of a glacier, would be blessed as compared with death from disease, or from some shabby lowland accident. But the best death, quick and crystal-pure, set so glaringly open before us, is hard enough to face, even though we feel gratefully sure that we have already had happiness enough for a dozen lives.

But poor Stickeen, the wee, hairy, sleekit beastie, think of him! When I had decided to dare the bridge, and while I was on my knees chipping a hollow on the rounded brow above it, he came behind me, pushed his head past my shoulder, looked down and across, scanned the sliver and its approaches with his mysterious eyes, then looked me in the face with a startled air of surprise and concern, and began to mutter and whine; saying as plainly as if speaking with words, "Surely, you are not going into that awful place." This was the first time I had seen him gaze deliberately into a crevasse, or into my face with an eager, speaking, troubled look. That he should have recognized and appreciated the danger at the first glance

showed wonderful sagacity. Never
before had the daring midget seemed
to know that ice was slippery or that
there was any such thing as danger
anywhere. His looks and tones of
voice when he began to complain and
speak his fears were so human that I
unconsciously talked to him in sympathy as I would to a frightened boy,
and in trying to calm his fears perhaps in some measure moderated my
own. "Hush your fears, my boy," I
said, "we will get across safe, though
it is not going to be easy. No right
way is easy in this rough world. We
must risk our lives to save them. At
the worst we can only slip, and then

how grand a grave we will have, and by and by our nice bones will do good in the terminal moraine."

But my sermon was far from re-assuring him: he began to cry, and after taking another piercing look at the tremendous gulf, ran away in desperate excitement, seeking some other crossing. By the time he got back, baffled of course, I had made a step or two. I dared not look back, but he made himself heard; and when he saw that I was certainly bent on crossing he cried aloud in despair. The danger was enough to daunt anybody, but it seems wonderful that he should have been able to weigh and appreciate it so justly. No mountaineer could have seen it more quickly or judged it more wisely, discriminating between real and apparent peril.

When I gained the other side, he screamed louder than ever, and after running back and forth in vain search for a way of escape, he would return to the brink of the crevasse above the bridge, moaning and wailing as if in the bitterness of death. Could this be the silent, philosophic Stickeen? I shouted encouragement, telling him the bridge was not so bad as it looked, that I had left it flat and safe for his feet, and he could walk it easily. But

he was afraid to try. Strange so small
an animal should be capable of such
big, wise fears. I called again and
again in a reassuring tone to come on
and fear nothing; that he could come
if he would only try. He would hush
for a moment, look down again at the
bridge, and shout his unshakable con-
viction that he could never, never
come that way; then lie back in despair, as if howling, "O-o-oh! what a
place! No-o-o, I can never go-o-o
down there!" His natural composure
and courage had vanished utterly in
a tumultuous storm of fear. Had
the danger been less, his distress
would have seemed ridiculous. But in

this dismal, merciless abyss lay the shadow of death, and his heartrending cries might well have called Heaven to his help. Perhaps they did. So hidden before, he was now transparent, and one could see the workings of his heart and mind like the movements of a clock out of its case. His voice and gestures, hopes and fears, were so perfectly human that none could mistake them; while he seemed to understand every word of mine. I was troubled at the thought of having to leave him out all night, and of the danger of not finding him in the morning. It seemed impossible to get him to venture. To compel him to try

through fear of being abandoned, I
started off as if leaving him to his fate,
and disappeared back of a hummock;
but this did no good; he only lay down
and moaned in utter hopeless misery.
So, after hiding a few minutes, I went
back to the brink of the crevasse and in
a severe tone of voice shouted across
to him that now I must certainly leave
him, I could wait no longer, and that,
if he would not come, all I could pro-
mise was that I would return to seek
him next day. I warned him that if he
went back to the woods the wolves
would kill him, and finished by urg-
ing him once more by words and gestures to come on, come on.

Stickeen

He knew very well what I meant, and at last, with the courage of despair, hushed and breathless, he crouched down on the brink in the hollow I had made for my knees, pressed his body against the ice as if trying to get the advantage of the friction of every hair, gazed into the first step, put his little feet together and slid them slowly, slowly over the edge and down into it, bunching all four in it and almost standing on his head. Then, without lifting his feet, as well as I could see through the snow, he slowly worked them over the edge of the step and down into the next and the next in succession in the

same way, and gained the end of
the bridge. Then, lifting his feet with
the regularity and slowness of the
vibrations of a seconds pendulum, as
if counting and measuring *one-two-
three*, holding himself steady against
the gusty wind, and giving separate
attention to each little step, he gained
the foot of the cliff, while I was on my
knees leaning over to give him a lift
should he succeed in getting within
reach of my arm. Here he halted in
dead silence, and it was here I feared
he might fail, for dogs are poor climb-
ers. I had no cord. If I had had one,
I would have dropped a noose over
his head and hauled him up. But while

Stickeen

I was thinking whether an available
cord might be made out of clothing,
he was looking keenly into the series
of notched steps and finger-holds I
had made, as if counting them, and
fixing the position of each one of
them in his mind. Then suddenly up
he came in a springy rush, hooking
his paws into the steps and notches so
quickly that I could not see how it
was done, and whizzed past my head,
safe at last!

And now came a scene! "Well
done, well done, little boy! Brave
boy!" I cried, trying to catch and ca-
ress him; but he would not be caught.
Never before or since have I seen

anything like so passionate a revulsion from the depths of despair to exultant, triumphant, uncontrollable joy. He flashed and darted hither and thither as if fairly demented, screaming and shouting, swirling round and round in giddy loops and circles like a leaf in a whirlwind, lying down, and rolling over and over, sidewise and heels over head, and pouring forth a tumultuous flood of hysterical cries and sobs and gasping mutterings. When I ran up to him to shake him, fearing he might die of joy, he flashed off two or three hundred yards, his feet in a mist of motion; then, turning suddenly, came back in a wild rush and launched himself at my face, almost knocking me down, all the time screeching and screaming and shouting as if saying, "Saved! saved! saved!" Then away again, dropping suddenly at times with his feet in the air, trembling and fairly sobbing. Such passionate emotion was enough to kill him. Moses' stately song of triumph after escaping the Egyptians and the Red Sea was nothing to it. Who could have guessed the capacity of the dull, enduring little fellow for all that most stirs this mortal frame? Nobody could have helped crying with him!

But there is nothing like work for

toning down excessive fear or joy. So I ran ahead, calling him in as gruff a voice as I could command to come on and stop his nonsense, for we had far to go and it would soon be dark. Neither of us feared another trial like this. Heaven would surely count one enough for a lifetime. The ice ahead was gashed by thousands of crevasses, but they were common ones. The joy of deliverance burned in us like fire, and we ran without fatigue, every muscle with immense rebound glorying in its strength. Stickeen flew across everything in his way, and not till dark did he settle into his normal fox-like trot. At

last the cloudy mountains came in
sight, and we soon felt the solid rock
beneath our feet, and were safe. Then
came weakness. Danger had vanished, and so had our strength. We
tottered down the lateral moraine
in the dark, over boulders and tree
trunks, through the bushes and devil-
club thickets of the grove where we
had sheltered ourselves in the morning, and across the level mud-slope
of the terminal moraine. We reached
camp about ten o'clock, and found a
big fire and a big supper. A party of
Hoona Indians had visited Mr. Young,
bringing a gift of porpoise meat and
wild strawberries, and Hunter Joe

nad prought in a wild goat. But we
lay down, too tired to eat much, and
soon fell into a troubled sleep. The
man who said, " The harder the toil,
the sweeter the rest," never was pro-
foundly tired. Stickeen kept spring-
ing up and muttering in his sleep,
no doubt dreaming that he was still
on the brink of the crevasse; and
so did I, that night and many others
long afterward, when I was over-
tired.

Thereafter Stickeen was a changed
dog. During the rest of the trip, instead of holding aloof, he always lay
by my side, tried to keep me con-
stantly in sight, and would hardly

accept a morsel of food, however
tempting, from any hand but mine.
At night, when all was quiet about
the camp-fire, he would come to me
and rest his head on my knee with a
look of devotion as if I were his god.
And often as he caught my eye he
seemed to be trying to say, "Was
n't that an awful time we had together on the glacier?"

Nothing in after years has dimmed
that Alaska storm-day. As I write it
all comes rushing and roaring to
mind as if I were again in the heart
of it. Again I see the gray flying
clouds with their rain-floods and

snow, the ice-cliffs towering above
the shrinking forest, the majestic ice-
cascade, the vast glacier outspread
before its white mountain fountains,
and in the heart of it the tremendous
crevasse,—emblem of the valley of
the shadow of death,—low clouds
trailing over it, the snow falling into
it; and on its brink I see little Stickeen, and I hear his cries for help and
his shouts of joy. I have known many
dogs, and many a story I could tell
of their wisdom and devotion; but to
none do I owe so much as to Stickeen. At first the least promising and
least known of my dog-friends, he
suddenly became the best known of

them all. Our storm-battle for life brought him to light, and through him as through a window I have ever since been looking with deeper sympathy into all my fellow mortals.

None of Stickeen's friends knows what finally became of him. After my work for the season was done I departed for California, and I never saw the dear little fellow again. In reply to anxious inquiries his master wrote me that in the summer of 1883 he was stolen by a tourist at Fort Wrangel and taken away on a steamer. His fate is wrapped in mystery. Doubtless he has left this

Stickeen

world — crossed the last crevasse —,
and gone to another. But he will not
be forgotten. To me Stickeen is im-
mortal.

NOTES

PAGE

xxiii   **J. G. Holland.** Josiah Gilbert Holland was
an American author and editor who was born
in 1819 and died in 1881. He was for many
years editor of *Scribner's Monthly*, which after-
wards became the *Century Magazine*.

3   **Fort Wrangel.** Now generally spelled Wran-
gell. Any good map of Alaska will show its
location.

Rev. S. H. Young. Samuel Hall Young, now
superintendent of Alaska Presbyterian missions
with office in New York City, but at that time a
missionary in the field with headquarters at
Fort Wrangel. Mr. Muir's *Travels in Alaska*
contains an interesting account of a mountain-
climbing adventure in which Mr. Young nearly
lost his life. Dr. Young (he received the degree
of D.D. in 1899) has written entertainingly of
this and other experiences with John Muir
(*Outlook*, May 26, June 23, and July 28, 1915).
In the last of his three articles he tells about
Stickeen, the subject of this story.

6   **Tail . . . shady as a squirrel's.** The Greek
word for squirrel, *skiouros*, from which our English word is derived, is formed from two words
meaning " shadow " and " tail." It is quite
likely that Mr. Muir had this in mind.

10   **The water was phosphorescent.** Some of the
small and microscopic animal life of the sea be-
comes luminous at night when disturbed by the
breaking of the waves, the churning of a boat's
propeller, the splashing of oars, the strokes of a
swimmer, or any similar cause, as, in this case,
the movements of the salmon. The surrounding
water at such times glows and sparkles beauti-
fully.

Notes

The salmon were running. Salmon, though for most of the year living in the sea, spawn only in fresh running water, and every spring and summer they swarm up the streams to the breeding-grounds. This is the time when they are caught for sport and for the market, — in the East by rod and line, in Alaska, where they are found in vast numbers, with nets and spears. This migration up the streams is called "running."

13 **Panax.** *Panax horridus*, or *Fatsia horrida*, a dangerously prickly araliaceous shrub commonly called devil's-club. It is abundant in Alaska.

Rubus. The genus of plants to which the blackberry, raspberry, cloudberry, and salmonberry belong.

15 **Wild-weathery.** One looks in the dictionaries in vain for this word, but its meaning is obvious. Mr. Muir was rather fond of coining playful words of this kind, such as are so common in his native Scotch.

16 **Diogenes.** A celebrated Greek Cynic philosopher who despised riches and is said to have lived in a tub. Plutarch relates that when Alexander the Great asked Diogenes whether he could do anything for him he replied, "Yes, I would have you stand from between me and the sun."

17 **Sphinx.** "A sphinxlike person; one of enigmatical or inscrutable character and purposes" (Webster's *New International Dictionary*). The Sphinx of Greek mythology propounded a riddle to all comers and, upon the failure of each one to guess it, speedily devoured him.

Tahkou. An Indian name, also spelled Taku.

Fountain ice-fields. The ice-fields that formed the sources of the glaciers.

[76]

Notes

PAGE

18   **Glacier Bay.** The famous Muir Glacier, discovered by Mr. Muir in 1879, is at the head of this bay.

    Yosemite. The Yosemite Valley of California, where Mr. Muir made his home for years.

22   **Storms.** John Muir was never afraid of bad weather. One of his most interesting papers is the account in *The Mountains of California* of how he climbed a tree in the forest during a wind-storm and remained there rocked wildly in the treetop while he studied the habits of the trees under such conditions.

26   **Dislocated his arm.** See the account in *Travels in Alaska.*

    Doggedly. Note the play on the word.

    "Where thou goest I will go." Doubtless suggested by Ruth's reply to her mother-in-law, Naomi, " Whither thou goest, I will go " (Ruth i, 16).

33   **Narrow tacks.** The word " tacks " is used in the nautical sense, as when a sailing vessel " tacks " to windward, taking a zigzag course because it is impossible to sail directly against the wind. By " narrow tacks " the author evidently means tacks in which little real progress was made, the crevasses coming very close together.

36   **Fountains.** In the sense of sources; in this case the sources of glaciers.

37   **Icebergs.** Icebergs are, of course, the natural discharge of a glacier into a lake or the sea.

54   **Power beyond our call or knowledge.** This has been the experience of many who have extricated themselves from imminent dangers by their own unaided efforts. The emergency calls forth hitherto unsuspected supplies of reserve energy.

Notes

PAGE

55   **Wee, hairy, sleekit beastie.** This reminds one of Burns's poem " To a Mouse," which begins " Wee, sleekit, cow'rin', tim'rous beastie." " Sleekit " is doubtless used in its original sense of sleek, smooth. It is the past participle of the verb " to sleek." Muir was fond of dropping occasionally into his native Scotch, especially when an affectionate diminutive was called for.

57   **We will get across safe.** Here and at the top of the next page Mr. Muir follows the Scotch custom of using the word " will " where the best English usage demands " shall."

69   **Devil-club.** See note on Panax, p. 76.

QUESTIONS AND
SUGGESTIONS

[79]

Questions

Questions

www.ingramcontent.com/pod-product-compliance
Lightning Source LLC
LaVergne TN
LVHW061226060426
835509LV00012B/1448